A HEARTBEAT from HELL…
…a choice for LIFE!

the STEVE MAYS story

Dedication

This booklet is dedicated to Arthur and Helen Mays (my mom and dad), who had to put up with me yet never gave up on me during the challenging years of my life. To my dad (who is in heaven), I am grateful for his wit and teaching me the importance of simplicity. To my precious mother, I am indebted to you forever. You taught me how to be gracious and giving and, most important, how to live unselfishly for others. It was my parents' exemplary lives and the lessons they imparted to me that have helped me, my family, and ministry. For them I thank the Lord!

TABLE OF CONTENTS

At one point in his life, Steve Mays was desperate, hopeless, and sleeping in gutters. He was living with a group of guys twice his age, who were involved in motorcycle gangs. A .38-caliber bullet had penetrated his left leg. The authorities wanted Steve for questioning regarding a recent shooting. Then one day something happened; Steve became a new man. His whole life changed.

It has been more than 30 years since the day Steve was sleeping in the gutter. Yet for the past 30 years, this man has been living a transformed life by the grace of God. God restored his soul, healed his mind and heart, and has been using him ever since, even in the midst of many difficult and painful experiences. Today, Steve Mays is the senior pastor of one of the largest churches in Los Angeles County.

This booklet was birthed from the life story of a man who at one point was *a heartbeat from hell* but by God's grace made a choice for life. Steve Mays has learned, and continues to learn to this day, that God has a wonderful plan and purpose for all people who choose life.

How can God love a desolate man full of anger and wrath? How can God take an addict and make him an obedient, God-fearing pastor? How can God use us to His fullest if we are weak or disabled?

In a day and age in which more people are living in gutters, nursing addictions, or struggling to survive on a daily basis, it seems as if there are few answers.

Many people are disillusioned and are filled with apathetic cynicism. They have lost hope and even sometimes question if life is worth living. Have you ever thought these thoughts, felt the pain of rejection, or experienced the emptiness of loneliness? Have you ever asked these questions: Am I too far gone? Is there hope for me? Will I make it? Will God see me through?

Regardless of what is taking place right now in your life, meditate on these truths: God's thoughts for you are more than all the sands of the sea (Psalm 139:17–18), and God desires to work in your life (Philippians 1:6). The story of God's work in a man like Steve Mays is a testimony to these truths, even if at times you believe you are a heartbeat from hell. *Will you choose life?*

The night was different from most others. It was mid-evening and surprisingly quiet, almost serene. Then suddenly, out of nowhere, a P-38 pistol was pointed right in the man's face.

Then came the voice. A familiar, sinister voice behind the gun clamored, "You're a dead man!" A slight pause, just for a second or two, then the angry voice behind the gun continued, "There's a contract out on your head, and I might as well collect on it before anyone else does!"

Immediately, he heard a deafening explosion that rang through his ears, followed by a searing pain like a red-hot iron ripping through the calf of his left leg. Screaming in horrific pain, he finally passed out on the floor.

The man awoke to a strange noise, discovering that he had no idea where he was. As he tried to get up, pain riveted his entire body. Still in a daze, he looked around. The surroundings were unfamiliar to him. Soon he realized he was lying in some strange field. Someone must have dumped him here.

Still in a daze, he knew he must have been drugged with large doses of "Reds" (barbiturates) to sedate him. He tried to sit up and grabbed for his leg. The muscles of his calf had been blown out. The blood had dried, and the pain was excruciating. Out of the gaping wound in his leg he pulled some bloody cloth rags that had been placed there to stop the bleeding. Pain shot throughout his body again.

"This is it!" he thought as he slumped back down in the dirt. The pain was unbearable. Then more disturbing thoughts came. There is no way to get out of this mess. There is no one to help and nowhere to go.

The FBI wanted him. Those he had called friends were the ones who had betrayed him, and he was unable to return home to his real family because of his horrible and explosive behavior. As he lay there looking up, his life passed before his eyes.

Steve Mays now longed for someone to help him, but there was no one—nowhere to go, and no one to call.

He was a sight to behold—weighing a meager 130 pounds, wearing dirty bib overalls, and having long matted hair weaved into a ponytail and earrings in his ear put in by a hammer and a 16-penny nail (about four inches long). He had an eight-inch goatee, which was tightly wrapped by three rubber bands. He had not bathed or brushed his teeth in months, and he had not slept soundly for weeks. In the evenings he would find safety in some filthy gutter between the concrete curb and a car door.

At that moment Steve thought to himself, *"I am going to die, and no one cares!"* He had to get his leg taken care of but could not think of one person who wanted him or who would help him. He knew that he could not go to a hospital because the authorities wanted Steve for questioning. He couldn't go home because his parents would call the authorities. Then, the pain being so intense, he passed out again there in the field, ready to die.

Chapter 1

BEYOND HOPE?

Stephen Mays was an ordinary kid who grew up in a large city in California. He was a fun-loving, all-American boy who earned good grades and had a bright future ahead of him. Steve had a passion for sports. He enjoyed football, but baseball was his passion. He excelled in the sport, playing shortstop and having a .450 batting average.

That day, a respected authority figure, a schoolteacher, had sexually molested him.

Yet despite a good upbringing and a wholesome family life, there was a day in Steve's life that changed everything. It was one of those days he wished would somehow go away forever, but instead, it made a powerful devastating impact, forcing his life into a downward spiral of anger, guilt, and horrible shame. It was the day his innocence was taken from his life forever.

Looking back, Steve pinpoints that one day in his life as his turning point toward destruction. He came home from school that day a changed person. The light went out from his life. His eyes darkened; his behavior became hostile. Yet no one could figure out what had happened to him.

That day, a respected authority figure, a schoolteacher, had sexually molested him. The teacher took him off campus by promising him extra credit for helping with a project. As soon as they were distanced from the school, the teacher told him to take off his clothes. Steve knew he was in danger. He was even more horrified when the teacher took out a camera. Afraid the teacher would harm him, Steve just did what his teacher told him to do. He was crying in his heart, desperately wanting the whole situation to go away.

Steve's life became marred. Hatred and bitterness began to grow. He couldn't understand why anyone in authority would lie and take advantage of him. He began to turn on all those who represented authority, even his parents. Steve had no idea how to deal with the pain that he was feeling inside. No matter what attempts he made to erase what had happened, the filthiness and shame continued to haunt him. In one moment everything had changed. He went from being a happy kid excited about life to being filled with resentment and anger.

As with most abuse victims, Steve remembers thinking that he had in some way brought this upon himself. Perhaps he was being punished for something he had done wrong.

Devastated, he felt like his life had come to an end. His safe, innocent, and happy world had been shattered.

Now filled with anger and hatred toward people, especially those in authority, Steve began rebelling. In a short time, he was smoking pot and stealing. His grades went from straight As to Ds and Fs. He lost all motivation for living. Steve did all he could to move on, trying to put the entire incident behind him and to forget what had happened. He didn't take anything serious anymore. Life became one big game that consisted mainly of cutting class; using pot, pills, and speed; and going to beach parties. Steve was on a twisted path toward destruction.

In the midst of trying to forget what had happened, the bitterness grew. He continued to push the anger and the feelings deep inside. How could he ever trust an adult again? If a teacher could do this and get away with it, then how many other kids did teachers abuse? Steve felt like he could tell and trust no one, not even his parents. In fact, his parents became targets for Steve to unload on. He became so violent that his parents resorted to calling the police when things got out of control. By the time he was in high school, these occasions had become common occurrences.

After a long string of rebellious and violent actions, Steve's crowning act took place one evening when he was home alone. When his parents returned, they had to shove open the front door because it had been wedged shut with towels. They discovered that their house had been made into a gigantic indoor bathtub. When they finally managed to open the front door, water came gushing out. As they looked around, they discovered their son sitting in the middle of the living room, completely oblivious to the damage being done to his parents' home. When his parents demanded an explanation, Steve (who was attempting to smoke a pencil) explained to them that he was simply watching a TV show. Sadly, the TV had never been turned on. Steve had been stoned for multiple hours on yet another chemical. By the time the police arrived, his parents had gotten him to his room. While in his room, Steve began to hallucinate. He saw the window hinges turn into toads. These toads spoke to him, and before long they were apparently telling him jokes and making him laugh. When the police officers found out that Steve was a member of the high school football team, they lectured him but did not arrest him.

> *They discovered that their house had been made into a gigantic indoor bathtub.*

At noon the next day, Steve's father returned home early from work to have a look at his less-than-model son. Steve was in the kitchen fixing two servings of milk and sandwiches. When asked whom the other sandwich was for, Steve motioned and pointed to the clock hanging on the wall. He tried to explain to his dad that the other sandwich was for Brad, the boy in the clock. Steve asked, "Don't you see his face in the clock? Can't you hear him? He's talking to us right now!" This was more than his dad could handle; he came to the conclusion that his son was crazy and hopeless.

Not long after this episode, Steve, stoned as ever (this time on LSD, marijuana, and a combination of other drugs), terrorized his parents with a machete. His mother looked on in horror as Steve, machete in hand, grimaced and paced around the house like a madman swinging the blade. When Steve fell asleep, his bewildered parents quietly took away the machete.

> *His mother looked on in horror as Steve, machete in hand, grimaced and paced around the house like a madman swinging the blade.*

Steve's father was a lab technician, a former military man, and a patriot. He had long come to the realization that his "60's generation" son had become impossible. The two had ceased communicating years before, and now the distance was as wide as the Grand Canyon. Deep down inside, Steve's pain was unbearable. He longed for his father to tell him that he loved him, but how? How could he express this longing to his dad? Furthermore, how could his father love someone who had done so much wrong?

To maintain his drug habit, Steve had to steal. His parents were called four different times to bring him down to the police station. Steve had broken into cars on his own street stealing tape decks. He had also become the school drug dealer and was kicked off the high school football team.

Shortly after Steve left the team, a few of the football players went up to the mountains to party. It was the first time that Steve's mom put her foot down and insisted that he couldn't go. For some reason Steve actually obeyed. The guys who went to the mountains got high on "Reds" (barbiturates) and overdosed. The mountain cabin they were staying in caught on fire, and some of them were unable to get out alive. This tragedy shook the entire high school. Steve's life was spared because he had stayed home, yet unfortunately the tragedy did nothing to jar him out of his destructive lifestyle. Instead, this event added more hurt and deep pain for Steve to bury down deep inside.

> *The mountain cabin...caught on fire, and some of them were unable to get out alive.*

Steve hated his life. He hated the person he had become and saw no hope for his future. He was ready to "check out." One by one, Steve had pushed away everyone who had once been important to him, especially his parents. He now completely despised them and totally turned against them. Hooked on "uppers" (methamphetamines), Steve was awake three to four days straight. As a result, he was a mental wreck.

Furthermore, Steve became extremely paranoid and turned toward revenge, a typical side effect of drugs.

Wanting to make sure people paid for what had happened in his life, Steve's rage caused him to be in frequent fights. In one particular battle, he went ballistic on a fellow high school student. He continued to beat him over and over again until other students pulled him off of the poor teen. At times, Steve wanted to punch anything or anyone just to relieve the inward shame and guilt.

As far as his parents were concerned, they had an incorrigible rebel on their hands who was beyond hope.

Chapter 2

THE GANG

Steve now did what he thought he had to do—run away. He wanted to run away from the pain and difficulty but, instead, ran straight into Satan's hands.

One day Steve came across a group of guys riding Harley-Davidson motorcycles. He was enticed and drawn toward this particular group of criminals. The motorcycle gang members were in their mid-30s, twice Steve's age. They carried guns and were heavily involved in crime and drug dealing. They were all tough guys; for example, they would shoot dogs just for laughs. Steve was innocent and calm in comparison to his new "friends." It was a match made in hell. He was invited to live with them and was able to stay as long as he worked on their bikes. Steve found a home in the hangout of that motorcycle gang, but he soon discovered a terror that he never would have dreamed existed in this home of criminals. Steve found

He found a home in the hangout of that motorcycle gang.

himself trapped in a demonic environment that most people don't know about or would ever want to know about.

The empty lives of these gang members were steeped in the drug counterculture of the day. The days were spent using, buying, and selling drugs, as well as other criminal activities. Pleasure was their motto.

Steve experienced many frightening incidents with the gang. However, one night's set of events stands out in particular:

> During this time, I would stay up all through the night and separate nuts and bolts and put them in order. Then I would dump them all out on the floor and work through this same ritual over and over again. That was how stoned I was.

> One night a motorcycle was tipped over. The gang members woke me up early that morning after my drug binge was over. They said that I had pushed one of their bikes over on to the ground. I explained that I didn't touch it and would never do something like that to them.

> One guy who had it in for me reached for something. It was then that I saw the blue barrels of a 12-gauge double shotgun as the others held me down. He told me to open my mouth, and he shoved the shotgun down my throat. I somehow said, "That isn't loaded,

is it?" Then he pulled the gun out of my mouth, pointed it at the pillow next to my ear, and pulled the trigger. It blew a hole in the mattress. Then they stuck the shotgun back in my mouth, and smoke began to come out. I thought I was going to die. To my surprise they pulled the shotgun out, then began to laugh sadistically. I was mentally and emotionally a basket case after that experience. My paranoia really began to grow from then on. I started carrying a gun when another guy living in the house felt sorry for me and gave me his gun to protect myself. I would stay awake all night just to make sure that I wouldn't die, because I was living in the same house with a guy who wanted to kill me.

Shortly after that first incident, I was in the backyard working on my own motorcycle that I had acquired. I was using a gasoline can as a chair while I worked on the bike. The same guy came out in the yard with a P-38 pistol and shot three rounds into the bottom of the can. Each shot missed me, and it was just a miracle that the gas can did not blow up with me on it.

Despite the terror, Steve did not leave the house. He was on a search to belong and to fit in, so he learned the lifestyle of his older "mentors" and became reckless with his new pistol. As the house members began to sell more and more drugs, Steve also began to deal. A girl came to the house to get drugs but refused to buy from Steve. When he asked her out, she said "no." Infuriated, he fired his gun at her when she started walking away. Fortunately, he was too stoned to hit her. The bullets flew over her head. She ran out of the house. Again his rage mounted. He now wanted to kill something, anything. The target became a cat. Steve describes what happened:

> I shot this alley cat with a P-38. It just smiled at me after I shot it. I felt sickened inside for doing it, but I just kept my feelings inside. From that point on, every place I went there was a cat. I think that was the closest I came to being demon-possessed.

A member of the gang told Steve that someone had taken a contract out on him, placing a price on his life. Instead of running, Steve got a shotgun with a 12-inch barrel and began practicing with it. With paranoia mounting and loneliness engulfing him, Steve kept taking drugs in an effort to dull the pain and block out his sadness.

A guy came up to Steve and pointed a P-38 pistol at him.

Then one evening while Steve was working on his bike, a man came up to Steve and pointed a P-38 pistol at him. He said, "You're a dead man!" There was a loud blast, and after Steve felt a searing pain in his leg, he passed out.

Chapter 3

THE OUTLAW

When Steve awoke, he found himself in a field. The pain from the gunshot wound was rapidly increasing. He knew he needed help, yet he realized that the only place he had to turn was the same house in which he had been shot! Steve decided that he would take his chances and go back to the house. The worst thing that could happen now is that the gang would kill him, but maybe someone might help him. He knew that if he lay there any longer he would die anyway. So in agony he struggled back to the house.

Steve pleaded, begged, and cried, hoping the gang members would get him help. Then Steve remembered a nurse his mother knew who lived just around the corner from his parents' home. They agreed to take him to the home of this nurse. Then to silence her and to keep her from giving him away, he threatened to kill her. She cleaned the wound and dried blood. Yet he needed further care. By his third visit to her, she finally got the courage to call his parents. Steve's mother called the FBI while he was still at the house getting his leg cleaned. When Steve and several members of the gang pulled away from the nurse's house in their car, they knew something was up.

Steve describes what looked liked a hopeless predicament:

I hadn't been home in years. So the authorities used a neighbor's house as a stakeout location. As we headed out of the nurse's house, I noticed a red Mustang making a U-turn. For once we weren't armed and had no dope. Two guys were in the front seat, and I was in the back. The pursuit began.

They surrounded us with rifles and shotguns and shouted, "If you move, you're dead!"

As we slowed down for a red light, the Mustang ran into the rear of our car, sending us careening into the middle of the intersection where three other cop cars suddenly wedged into us. They surrounded us with rifles and shotguns and shouted, "If you move, you're dead!" They pulled me out of the backseat and kicked my legs apart in order to search me. I can still remember the gun being held to my head and the shotguns aimed at us. Once again I thought for sure that I was going to die. Before I knew it, the officers had slammed my face against the hood of my car, which in the 100-degree summer heat amplified the scorching pain. Then they handcuffed my ankles and my hands and threw me into the back of their car.

They realized they had me for draft evasion and thought they had apprehended me—the right suspect for shooting an old lady. I had been accused of shooting this lady during a robbery. She had told the authorities she returned fire with a rifle and hit the suspect with a .22-caliber bullet. Fortunately, it was clear I had been shot by a .38-caliber bullet.

Then the FBI let me go! All I was required to do was report to the draft board, which I did. To my surprise they also released me, not wanting to send me to Vietnam because of my gunshot wound. I never understood why either agency let me go. However, it is clear to me today that God was beginning to move in my life.

Even though being released by the FBI was a miracle, to a gang member it is probably the worst thing that could happen. To be the first one released normally meant you sold out your companions to secure your own freedom. Thus, the gang members were convinced that Steve had betrayed them. Therefore, they kicked Steve out of the gang house. Now Steve had no place to live. He began sleeping in gutters. Still suffering from drug-induced paranoia, he was now plagued with the possibility of being found, beaten up, or shot again, on the streets.

Chapter 4

A Clean Break

Being empty and wasted on life, relationships, and drugs, Steve's bitterness was deepening. He was sleeping in gutters unable to shower or get a good meal. Then one day a husband and wife named Henry and Shirley discovered Steve as they came out to their car, which was parked near the gutter in which Steve was sleeping. Amazingly they invited Steve into their home, gave him a long-overdue shower, and fed him a meal. Shirley saw hope for Steve and told him that she saw Jesus in his eyes.

Shirley and Henry had been on their way to their church, Calvary Chapel. They invited Steve to go with them. At this time Calvary Chapel was meeting in a small church building in Costa Mesa, California. It was very different from how Steve remembered church to be when he had attended as a child. There were swarms of young people—hippies just like Steve with long hair, bell-bottoms, and bare feet. The church was packed; many people were standing and some were even sitting on the floor. This place was different. Steve noticed that there were even businessmen, in their suits, embracing the hippies. What could these people possibly have in common? Everyone was hugging, and all had huge smiles on their faces. They didn't seem to be "high" but rather genuinely happy. Steve was compelled to be part of what was happening. He listened intently and, for the first time in years, was intrigued by this "authority figure."

This man was different, and right then I knew I wanted whatever it was that he had.

Steve remembers when the pastor, Chuck Smith, came out to greet everyone:

He wasn't at all what I imagined him to be; he seemed different from typical preachers. He had this huge smile that just captivated me, and for the first time I saw a man whom I admired. I saw in Pastor Chuck a strength that I had never seen before. He was built like a rock, and he spoke like a prophet of God! I saw a genuine love in his eyes. This man was different, and right then I knew I wanted whatever it was that he had!

Each word that Pastor Chuck spoke cut to Steve's heart. At the end of the service, Pastor Chuck gave an invitation. Anyone who wanted to know Jesus Christ as his or her Lord and personal Savior was called to go forward to the front of the church for prayer. Steve knew that this was what he needed. It was so different from anything he had tried before. He somehow knew that the love he was experiencing that night was supernatural; it could only be God! God was calling him and drawing him out of Satan's grip into His loving arms.

That night Steve accepted the salvation of Jesus Christ into his life. Henry and Shirley knew he needed to get off the streets. What Steve needed was a clean break and a chance to get his life back on the right track. Shirley called three different organizations; one of those was the Mansion Messiah House of Calvary Chapel.

Henry and Shirley took Steve to Mansion Messiah. He walked in with his gun stuck in the back of his pants. Steve recalls walking through the door of the Mansion Messiah home that night.

> Immediately, this little squirt named Orville looked right in my eyes and said, "Do you have a gun?" I said, "Yes." He then asked me for it and took it from me. Then he asked me, "Do you know Jesus?" I was nervous, so I said, "No." All I could remember at that very moment was how big his Bible was. It was a large Thompson Chain Reference Bible, and all I had was a little tiny, tiny gun. I kept thinking to myself, *Look at the size of his Bible.* He said, "Bow your head, Steve; we're going to ask Jesus into your heart right now." I then remember bowing my head and praying with him.

Orville didn't preach at him, he didn't give a big sermon, and he didn't even try to explain a plan of salvation or the Gospel. He simply had Steve repeat a simple prayer asking Jesus to be his Lord and Savior.

That night Steve became a new man. It was as if God just grabbed him and reached deep into his heart. It was the most incredible power he had ever experienced. For the first time in many years, Steve knew he was truly loved.

When Steve went to bed that night, he knew he was a different man. He felt loved like he never had before, and he knew he belonged somewhere. He no longer felt rejected by society, and he no longer had a chip on his shoulder. The love of Christ had penetrated his soul. That night, however, he was also reminded that although he was forgiven, there were still consequences to his sinful past. In a vivid vision from the Lord, Steve could see his face in the crossbeam of a rifle scope. The person holding the gun pulled the trigger, and the bullet left the barrel. In terror, Steve cried out to God. Suddenly he saw a hand holding a U-pipe. The bullet went straight into the pipe, turned around, and killed his stalker. Steve believes the one shooting the gun was Satan.

> *The bullet went straight into the pipe, turned around, and killed his stalker.*

What a vision! At this moment Steve clearly realized there would be a battle in his life. Satan, his own mind, and life itself would constantly try to remind Steve of his sinful past. That same night, however, Steve read a Scripture that would guide him for life: "Greater is He who is in you than he who is in the world" (1 John 4:4, NASB). As he awoke from this horrible dream and powerful vision, Steve knew God had filled his heart and life and would use him in the ministry one day.

Although the change in Steve's life was instantaneous, he had no idea what it meant to live as a Christian. In one day he was a completely different person, but he still had many habits to change. He remembers opening a beer the next day and one of the workers telling him, "Steve, you are a Christian now; we don't get drunk." Later he went outside to light a joint and another told him, "You are a Christian, and Christians don't smoke pot." While running some errands with another resident from the house, Steve noticed some good-looking girls and suggested that they pick them up. But he was told that as a Christian he shouldn't be trying to pick up girls any more and that sex outside of marriage was a sin. It was this *one-on-one discipleship* that helped Steve grow in his walk with the Lord.

Steve knew that God had delivered him from drugs, destruction, and himself. He flushed the drugs down the toilet. He also threw his guns into the ocean. The residents of Mansion Messiah buried his clothes because they smelled so bad!

God wanted to free Steve of a lot of baggage. He had grown so bitter at the world and especially toward those in positions of authority. He knew that the pieces of his life would be put back together one step and one day at a time. God placed it on Steve's heart to start putting the pieces back together by first making amends with his parents. He had grown to hate them and had blamed them for just about everything. For the first time in years, Steve telephoned his mom. He told her that he had accepted Jesus Christ and described the events that had taken place. His mom responded to him by saying, "Anything that can change you, I want right now!" She accepted the Lord right then over the phone.

When his father was dying of cancer in the hospital, Steve could no longer hold back from discussing Christ with him.

Steve then apologized and witnessed to his dad. His dad, however, wasn't as convinced as his mom was. His dad had grown tired of Steve's explosive behavior and his many passing fads. So he told Steve, "I don't want to hear about it. I want to see it in your life first." So for the next 17 years, Steve just lived a changed life before his dad. When his father was dying of cancer in the hospital, Steve could no longer hold back from discussing Christ with him. Steve again shared Christ with his dad, and God moved powerfully in his dad's heart. Steve's dad accepted Jesus Christ as his Lord and Savior that day. Eventually Steve's brother, Gary, and Gary's wife, Judy, even came to know the Lord.

Chapter 5

A CALLING

The 1970s were a special time for many young people like Steve. Hippies were coming to know Jesus Christ as their Lord and personal Savior in droves. In fact, newspapers and magazines reported on what was taking place at Calvary Chapel.

These young hippies soon became known as the "Jesus People." Because of the radical transformation that had occurred in their lives, the surrounding communities could not help but notice that something was going on. Almost overnight these lost hippies were flushing their drugs down the toilet and making a fresh start. Many found the love and purpose for which they had been so desperately searching.

Calvary Chapel Costa Mesa soon outgrew its small building and began making plans for a larger church facility. In the meantime the church bought a huge tent, which became its new sanctuary. Every night thousands of hippies showed up, and there would be contemporary music and a Bible study from Pastor Chuck.

Pastor Chuck's heart ached to reach this lost generation, not with rules and religion but simply with love, grace, and God's Word. He believed these young people needed teaching, not preaching. So he began teaching them the Bible, chapter by chapter and verse by verse. Pastor Chuck's philosophy was (and still is today) that if he simply taught the Bible as the whole counsel of God, then God would do the work of changing lives from the inside out.

Calvary Chapel Costa Mesa also realized that many of these hippies needed a place to make a fresh start, an environment for them to get their lives straightened out. Sending them back onto the streets would just encourage old habits again. Hence, the vision for the communal houses was borne.

In 1971 Steve, like many others, became a resident of a Christian communal house, where 20 to 30 young people would live together in a family-type setting. The home was exactly what Steve needed to get on the right track. Designed to bring purpose and structure to young lives, it was a valuable way for Steve to learn some well-needed discipline. The home was run with very strict guidelines: no TV, movies, or books except the Bible. Each home had a leader who would make sure these rules were followed. Everyone was expected to do their share. Established residents would submit their paychecks to help cover the home's expenses, while new residents (some who were coming off drugs) would help by maintaining the home and working in the lawn-mowing business.

This was a unique period in Steve's life, and he was determined to make the most of his new start. Like the other residents, Steve committed what spare time he had to intense Bible study and sharing his new faith with almost everyone he met. During this period, Steve heard God's voice clearly tell him that he had been called to full-time ministry in the Body of Christ.

He had years of cobwebs to clear from Steve's head due to years of drugs and rebellion.

This new revelation was almost too much for him to handle, but God's love was breaking through Steve's stubborn and rebellious heart. The Lord had a great deal of work to do in Steve's life. He had years of cobwebs to clear from Steve's head due to years of drugs and rebellion. Christian character had to be formed in Steve in a slow and costly way. There was no shortcut through this process.

Steve's first position of spiritual leadership came after he had spent more than two years in two different communal houses in Costa Mesa. Steve felt led by the Lord to go to the California desert area of Victorville and start a Christian communal house there. He called Pastor Chuck's brother Paul and soon learned that they had been praying for someone to start a commune in that exact area.

Steve was excited; before long, his desire and vision came to pass. A house in Victorville called the Macedonia House was started with a total of 30 residents. Of the 30, four of them became Calvary Chapel pastors sometime later.

One day in Victorville, as Steve was serving the Lord, an amazing thing happened. A pretty blonde girl passed right in front of Steve's eyes. She had long hair past her waist, with a flower by her ear. Steve recalls:

> I couldn't help but take a second look! Her face was aglow with the love of Jesus Christ. Her name was Gail. Then I heard the most bizarre thing. It was a voice that said, "This is your wife." I remember responding in my heart, "Satan, get thee behind me!"

Yet Steve knew that it was God speaking to him and that He had laid this woman upon his heart. Steve was stunned and speechless. Yet Gail was only visiting this Christian house. Her home was in Orange County.

That evening, Steve immediately began to question exactly what God was speaking to him. He knew there was something special about Gail. Deciding to search the Scriptures for answers, he opened his Bible and the pages fell open to Proverbs 18. The passage Steve immediately saw was Proverbs 18:22 (NASB): "He who finds a wife finds a good thing and obtains favor from the LORD."

Steve was still doubtful. He had been hurt by previous relationships and decided to put God to the test. He prayed,

"OK, Lord, if I call her and it just happens to be her birthday [as he had heard] and if no one is celebrating with her and in fact she is weeping over this, then I will believe."

Steve doubtfully called her. To his amazement, the situation played out exactly as he had asked. He said to her, "Do you want to come out to Victorville and spend time together?" Gail's response was, "I will be there within a couple of hours." And she left for Victorville immediately.

That evening they went out to dinner. Gail remembers thinking that Steve was too poor to eat as he ordered just a small bowl of soup, but in fact Steve was too nervous to eat. Gail thought he was going to invite her to stay in Victorville and help with the commune as one of the sisters in charge of the women. Instead, Steve proposed to her! To his shock, she accepted immediately. Steve recollects,

> The next day I called my mother and told her I was getting married. She was shocked, to say the least. She said, "Stephen, I just talked with you a week ago."
> "I know, Mom, but God has really spoken to my heart."
> "Stephen, what is her name?"
> "Gail," I said.
> "And her last name?"
> "Mom, I didn't ask her! I will call her and ask her right away!"

My poor mother probably wondered if I was back on drugs again.

In one week, Steve and Gail were married. Paul Smith, Pastor Chuck Smith's brother, performed the ceremony.

Not long after, Pastor Chuck Smith called Steve to pastor his first church in the desert of San Bernardino. The church was in the city of Twentynine Palms, and it was only miles from a military base filled with tough Marines. This was the last place on earth Steve wanted to go. The city was hot, barren, and full of tumbleweeds. Nevertheless, Steve showed up with his wife, his newborn son, and his ponytail.

Later, Steve would come to understand that God was preparing him during these desert years for greater ministry. Steve's thirst for God's Word became almost insatiable, and he began to build his own library of Bible commentaries (a collection he continues today). It was in this dry desert town that Steve began to experience the living water of God's Word.

However, despite this time of deep personal growth, Steve still experienced many disappointments while in Twentynine Palms. The small body of believers continued to appear dry and fruitless. Steve was forced to rely on the "strong arm" of the Lord and lean only on Him. It was at this time that another Scripture became a lifelong guide: "As your days, so shall your strength be" (Deuteronomy 33:25).

Chapter 6

TIME TO GROW

After years of discouragement in Twentynine Palms and being broken before God, Steve showed up at Calvary Chapel Costa Mesa looking for Pastor Chuck Smith. Finding him in the parking lot, Steve silently and brokenly dropped the keys to the Twentynine Palms church into his hands. The church had divided and finally closed. Steve thought that it was all over, that he would never be used in ministry again.

Both men just stood there in the parking lot looking at each other—Pastor Chuck no doubt wondering if this kid would ever make it; Steve wondering if God would ever trust him again. However, after this meeting, Steve departed and purposed in his heart that he would never quit again, no matter how difficult it got.

To Steve's great surprise, Pastor Chuck offered Steve a position as the elder of one of the Christian houses called the House of Psalms. The grace of God spoke through Pastor Chuck, giving this heartbroken young man another chance. Steve accepted the position. It was here that God did His breaking work in Gail. In Twentynine Palms they had been living in a three-bedroom house in a quiet neighborhood. Now she was sharing a cramped house with 40 other people. Their new kitchen became the meeting hall, leaving Gail to do her dishwashing in the bathtub.

More than one thousand people passed through those communal houses, and lives were being changed. It was a sacrifice that had eternal rewards. Steve and Gail lived and were involved with these homes for more than seven years.

After overseeing the communal homes, Steve started a church in Buena Park, now known as Calvary Chapel of Cypress. Two more years of additional trials and struggles ensued, during which they prayed the church would grow and be fruitful. Yet the Lord had impressed on Steve's heart the need for him to leave the church he had started; he believed God had said that he could never be an effective senior pastor until he learned the real lesson of submission. Steve knew one of the ways he could learn submission was in the role of an assistant pastor. So he left his church in Cypress, and for two years he became an assistant pastor at Hosanna Chapel. Steve felt that he had somehow lost his priorities and was now rededicating his life to the Lord. But he was also afraid that he didn't have the call or gifts to be a senior pastor. He had tried this twice and seemingly failed both times.

Right after leaving the church in Cypress, Steve received a very difficult phone call from Pastor Chuck. It was one of those phone calls a person wishes he never had to answer.

The voice came through the receiver, "Steve, this is Pastor Chuck. Why am I the last one to find out about you leaving your church?" Steve was stunned and silent. Chuck told him that a true shepherd never shocks the people; rather, he warns them. Chuck took the time to chasten Steve, sharing that he had shocked the people in Cypress and that a shepherd should never leave the way he did. Then Chuck finished his conversation with these last words, "Steve, you are not a shepherd. Next time call me first!"

Steve vividly recalls that conversation with Pastor Chuck and his ensuing feelings:

> I was devastated beyond belief! It was like God spoke to me over the phone. I was foolish and very immature in my actions, but there was hope. In all my tears and anguish, two words stood out like towers of hope in my life. The Holy Spirit must have shouted them into my heart. The two words were, "Next time." Yes, that is what Pastor Chuck said, "Next time." Then I remember thinking, *God, could there ever be a "next time"?*

God was not finished with Steve. Years went by. Steve finally gave up the thought of ever pastoring a church of his own. There were several occasions in his life when it looked like this would never happen. Steve's final stipulation to the Lord was, "Chuck Smith is going to have to personally call me with the position." At a place of desperation and brokenness, Steve finally let go and gave up the thought. He then went on a long overdue vacation.

On this vacation Steve went fishing. He started talking to the Lord again about pastoring and asked Him for some kind of sign: "If I am ever going to pastor again, Lord, I am going to have to catch a fish before this hook leaves the water." Steve started to reel his line in while the hook glinted under the surface. When the hook was about to break the top of the water, Steve's eyes welled up with tears. No fish would bite it now; it was too late. Yet just as the hook was coming out of the water, a tiny fish bit it. That tiny fish meant more to Steve than any five-pound bass. Steve knew God had heard his cry for a sign. He also felt God saying, "In a little while, I will speak to you again."

When Steve returned from his vacation, he got a message that he was to call Pastor Chuck or Pastor Don McClure. Returning the call, Steve was told that his name had been unanimously recommended during a regional pastors' meeting for a senior pastor position at Calvary Chapel South Bay in Los Angeles. Steve was so excited that he almost passed out.

In the spring of 1980, Steve walked onto the premises of his new church. That day there was a song in his heart, and Steve knew that this was the hand of the Lord.

Steve really wanted to make this work and to start things from scratch. He asked the Lord for the entire existing board of elders to resign so he could start fresh. And that is exactly what happened. Calvary Chapel South Bay was home at that time to a congregation of about 50 people, and they occupied a building of 1,500 square feet.

Within just a few years of ministry, the church had to move to a bigger facility nearby. The newer property was 15,000 square feet, and there were enough funds to remodel.

Through the years of failure, God had taught Steve about being faithful in the small things. What Steve had considered "failed attempts," God saw as great opportunities for Steve to grow. Steve learned that there is *absolutely nothing that comes into our lives that God hasn't allowed.* Through the book of Zechariah, Steve was reminded that the foundation of the new Temple had to be laid before the walls went up. God had to teach Zerubbabel

Through the years of failure, God had taught Steve about being faithful in the small things.

patience and not to "despise the day of small things" (see Zechariah 4:10). Steve, for a time, had been caught in that desire to build the walls before the foundation was laid. In this, he learned that it is vitally important not to build out of sequence but to dig deep and lay the foundation on the Rock. This new church would be Steve's opportunity to do God's work God's way, one day at a time!

Chapter 7

STILL LEARNING

God started doing a great work at Calvary Chapel South Bay. The church continued to grow. Soon, a newer main sanctuary of 14,000 square feet was needed. God was adding to the church quicker than Steve could get property. The only solution was to start building. Yet it was a big task, and Steve had only a small staff. It was only a matter of time before Steve found himself spending most of his waking hours working at or on the church. He recalls,

> The building project was a stretching time in my life. I remember doing the everyday church things, ministering, teaching, administration, and counseling. I was doing three services on Sunday mornings, one on Sunday nights, and a midweek study on Thursday nights. I complained so much to God. We didn't have a large pastoral staff at that point so I felt like I had more than I could handle. On top of this, we were building and trying to find space anywhere we could. Between the ministry and the construction projects, I was working day and night. I finally

realized one day that I was doing things with the wrong attitude. It was not pleasing to God. I wasn't doing it *for* God. I was doing it *for myself* and for everyone else.

God always gives us an opportunity to learn a lesson. Unfortunately, I didn't learn my lesson, and God wanted more in my life. He wanted more of me. I believe that because I didn't yield to Him, God allowed His instrument of sickness to come into my life.

One day Steve woke up and just couldn't get out of bed. Steve had always been an extremely active person; he was continually on the go. On this day, sick and weak, he felt like his whole world had caved in. All his strength and energy were gone. The doctors ran a lot of tests, including a brain scan. They diagnosed him to be suffering from a chronic illness known as Epstein-Barr; today it is called Chronic Fatigue Syndrome (CFS). CFS causes extreme fatigue, headaches, sore throats, muscle and joint aches, memory loss, and a whole range of other symptoms. It feels like a bad case of the flu that never gets better.

> *One day Steve woke up and just couldn't get out of bed.*

Steve tried fiercely to fight the condition, only to discover that he couldn't win. With his immune system severely compromised, Steve spent a lot of time recuperating and resting. Yet supernaturally the Lord gave him the strength to continue in the pulpit. Here are Steve's thoughts about this time:

> When I first got sick, I honestly didn't know if it was because of all the drugs I took in my past or because of all the stress. I had no energy, no ability to do anything. I was completely dependent on other people; Gail even had to drive me to church. I suffered from memory loss. I lost so much of my memory that I got frustrated with my whole situation. I eventually had no choice but to fall back on the fact that God had allowed this in my life and there was a purpose for it.

> Even though this was difficult to accept, it was a time when God really spoke to the depths of my heart. Through the writings of Amy Carmichael, I learned about the reality of ministry versus relationship. I had been living trying to please people all the time, and God wanted me to live every day with the desire of pleasing only Him. When God is put first, then everything else will fall into place.

> I was at the doctor's office at least once every week, for two years. It was such a humbling experience.

Many people could not relate to what I was going through. Many people believed that it was completely unacceptable for a pastor or spiritual leader to be sick. Unfortunately, some teach that chronic sickness occurs because of supposed hidden sin in one's life. I, however, realized that God wasn't punishing me but that He had allowed this. A key encouragement I received was through the example of Paul the apostle, who also had a thorn in his flesh. This was my thorn in the flesh, my opportunity to show those around me that in my weakness, God's strength is made perfect.

Today Steve realizes just how much he learned through this sickness. At the time, he longed for it to be over, but now he sees how the hand of God was there for him to lean on. It was a great time of learning for Steve. For the first time he was able to relate with those in his congregation who were sick. He could say from his heart that he understood what they were going through. He realized that all too often those who are sick are frequently cast aside. People just don't understand how to deal with them:

There were times when I didn't understand why people didn't reach out and help. Right or wrong, I realized that in the Body of Christ there isn't much compassion or love for people who are sick. We often don't know what to say and therefore don't reach out or love those who perhaps need it more than others. God may oftentimes use sicknesses for His glory. This was certainly true for my life.

As a result of his illness, Steve began to place a great emphasis on pastoral hospital visits for the sick and the families of the sick. He also learned a few key lessons. First, God wants to work in us, and this is more important to Him than working through us. Second, although His thoughts for us are many, He is more concerned about our character than our comfort.

When Steve was finally recovering from CFS, in 1993 tragedy struck. A pastor at Calvary Chapel South Bay, Bruce Bryan, was murdered. Bruce had been by Steve's side from the very beginning at Calvary Chapel South Bay. He even helped build the main sanctuary. Bruce had opened a men's home in the area and ministered the love of God to many young men caught up in drugs, alcohol, and gang violence. He was also involved in the Los Angeles County Sheriff Department's volunteer chaplain program and would frequently ride along with the deputies.

One night during a ride-along, the deputy and Bruce offered a wayward young man a ride home. Yet somehow, the young man managed to take the deputy's gun. He shot and wounded the deputy, then turned the gun on Bruce, shooting and fatally wounding him.

At the time of the shooting, Steve was in Florida ministering with Pastor Chuck at a church dedication. He returned immediately to find the press broadcasting the story on the Los Angeles television stations. It was an extremely difficult time for both Steve and the church. Steve recalls the aftermath:

> When Bruce was killed, it was a horrible thing. I still do not know how to handle a situation like that to this day. I can't help but have mixed emotions. I miss him dearly but have to believe that it was God's perfect timing for Bruce to go home. Every time he stepped into a police car, the possibility existed that something could happen. It was a reality that we had talked about but never dreamed would happen. God says that our days are numbered. It was Bruce's time. He went home to be with the Lord. I had to try to come to terms with the Lord's timing.
>
> This was a life-changing time in our church. We had to ask, "Why would God allow this?" But the real question was, "Why not?" Many have gone before us and have suffered for doing good works. Bruce made the ultimate sacrifice with his life. The Bible says "to be absent from the body is to be present with the Lord," and that's a glorious thing. Bruce is not in pain but in heaven rejoicing with his Lord. Instead of mourning him, we needed to celebrate his life.

In the midst of this difficulty, Steve's bouts with illness continued. In 1994, he severely injured his knee, which resulted in several surgeries. Unfortunately, these surgeries did not correct his knee problem. The pain became so great that it was difficult for him to stand and teach in the pulpit. Finally, doctors performed major reconstructive surgery on his knee, which left him bedridden for 40 days. Steve learned another valuable lesson during this time:

> Things were doing better at church, yet right in the middle of it all, God took me out. I didn't understand the wisdom of it. Why would He do this? And once again I realized that He wanted me to let go of *everything* I was hanging on to.

In 1995, Steve was diagnosed with severe sleep apnea. Shortly after the diagnosis, the doctors decided to do yet another surgery, this time on his throat to enlarge his esophagus and hopefully correct the problem he was having in sleeping. Steve remembers,

> The surgery's intent was to open up the passage and let more air in. It was a painful operation. During recovery, I remember throwing up blood at 1:00 A.M., in the kitchen where I fell to my knees, crying out to God.
>
> Again, I thought God was finished with me and that I was going to be put on the shelf. God showed me

that He never "shelves" people. There is always work to be done both inward and outward. There is always a battle to fight. I learned that at times we may be wounded, but we should always be soldiers.

From Amy Carmichael I learned that in bed and throughout illness, I could still pray. Although through her illness Amy couldn't get out of bed, she would visit countries in her prayers. With this perspective, I realized I had a lot of ground to make up.

Although the throat surgery was successful, Steve's sleeping problems continued. Sleep studies performed at UCLA Medical Center in Los Angeles revealed that Steve woke up about 150 times a night and never reached REM sleep.

In 1996, Steve again had surgery to remove a blockage in his nasal passage, which the doctor was convinced was responsible for his sleep problems. The surgery went well, and Steve seemed to be healing nicely. Then in late May, he planned a fishing trip with his worship pastor. It was going to be a great trip; it would be the first vacation he had in a long time, and he was going to do one of his favorite things—fish. The two left for Mexico.

While fishing, they had a great day; in fact, it was one of the best fishing days of his life. Steve caught an eight-foot sailfish and many other kinds of fish. However, that night, Steve began to hemorrhage. At first it seemed like a nosebleed, but he was actually hemorrhaging inside his nose. Blood was pouring down the back of his throat and through his nose. His blood pressure became abnormal, and of course in Mexico there were no doctors or hospitals around. Finally, they found a doctor who was able to sedate him, but they could not stop the bleeding.

About 2:00 A.M. that morning, Steve was taken in an ambulance to a small, hole-in-the-wall hospital. He was still bleeding, and all he could think about was his wife and kids. Miraculously, the doctor who came to care for him said that he'd just finished watching a video on how to stop this type of bleed.

Back home, after hearing about all these events, someone had anonymously made arrangements for a jet to fly into Mexico and pick up Steve. To this day he still has no idea who it was. The jet flew into Long Beach, California, and Steve was rushed straight to the hospital. During that long night he lost nearly two pints of blood.

> I thought I was going to die. The whole time I had been a Christian I had never feared death. I had always been this macho guy, not afraid of dying. But that night I was so afraid. The lesson I learned was that I did not want to die. I wanted to live. I finally understood the passage in Philippians where Paul described the same struggle and said "to live is Christ, and to die is gain" (Philippians 1:21). I wanted

> to be with my Lord, yet there was a conflict in that I wanted to live and be with my family. I wasn't sure that God was finished with me yet.

Steve recovered from this life-threatening emergency, but he wasn't out of the hospital for long. Soon thereafter he began suffering with pain, cramps, and nausea when he would eat. Late one night after a Sunday evening service, Steve had a gallbladder attack.

> That Sunday I taught in the worst pain I'd ever been in. I passed out, woke up, and went straight to the doctor, who put me right into the hospital. I was operated on within two hours. My gallbladder had ruptured. I remember asking, "Why, God, why?" And I remember God speaking to my heart, "Why not?" A peace came over me. The doctor told me that this would be a great surgery, that I'd be able to eat anything and not get sick.

The doctor, however, was wrong; Steve's problem was not solved. Unable to eat and in severe pain, he began to lose weight. The doctors were baffled and attempted to treat him a number of ways, but nothing seemed to work. Finally, they were forced to attempt a very serious operation. Steve returned to the hospital that year for an operation on his pancreas. He was told that the surgery entailed high risk. Furthermore, there was a chance he could be hospitalized for as long as six months. Steve went before his congregation a few days before the surgery and explained to the people, at the end of that evening's service, exactly what was going to happen. The board of elders laid hands on him that night and prayed over him. Many people prayed for Steve before, during, and after that surgery, and the Lord graciously answered those prayers. Steve not only came through the surgery successfully, but he was out of the hospital in a few days.

Through these ailments and surgeries, even up through today, Steve has been learning the importance of delegation. He has had to learn to trust his staff and let God do the work. Steve had always been a man who took pride in getting things done. But in these circumstances, there were times when he couldn't even get out of bed. Therefore, he was forced to delegate. He learned that if he didn't delegate, he would lose what God had given him. He had to let go and let God take over.

It was so amazing for Steve to see the church grow without him. It was painful to admit the truth, but the truth needed to be understood. God didn't need Steve Mays; rather, Steve Mays needed God! This was God's work, not Steve's, and God wanted to make sure he understood this lesson!

Through all these illnesses and trials, Steve has kept his sense of humor. As he has said on more than one occasion,

> When the apostle Paul went to a new city, he'd look for the prisons he'd be going to. When people go to new cities, they generally look for hotels. When I get to a new city, I look for hospitals!

A Heartbeat From Hell

Chapter 8

UNLESS HE BUILDS

In 1997 God wanted to multiply the ministry of Calvary Chapel South Bay. Through all the ailments, surgeries, pain, and difficulties, God was working changes in Steve's life. Now God wanted to manifest for others to see the fruit of what He had been doing inside of His servant Steve.

During this season, Steve was able to have lunch with internationally known author and teacher Alan Redpath, during one of his conferences in the United States. Steve can remember how empty he felt on the inside:

> I remember sharing this with Alan Redpath. His counsel to me was life-changing. He told me, "When you look in the mirror and all you see are tumbleweeds, remember this one truth: God has gone underground and is working on the root system of your life. One day the Holy Spirit will bring forth the new harvest in your life!" Alan's words were so profound for me.

With all that was going on in my heart, I couldn't help but ask one more question. I said, "Why is it that some teachers can continue to go on in the ministry even when they are not completely yielding to God?" Alan's answer was reviving yet convicting: "Stephen, it's like a train going down the tracks at 90 miles an hour. When the engineer turns off those mighty engines that pull the train, does the train stop? No way!" He said, "It continues, but the train loses speed every inch of the way until the moment it isn't moving anymore." I realized this was an incredible insight for me to learn. I need to keep the train moving through His grace and His love—and never give up.

The ministry of Calvary Chapel South Bay began to expand, and it was again time to find a new church location. The odds were definitely against them. Real estate prices were out of control. Available property of that size needed appropriate zoning, which is difficult to get in Los Angeles. Furthermore, Calvary Chapel South Bay had become a diverse ethnic and multicultural church ministering in an inner-city environment—not by any means an ideal risk as far as the banks were concerned. The people in the Carson area had loved and supported the church for many years. Neither Steve nor the board would ever desert them in lieu of finding a building elsewhere. Yet at the same time, Steve felt that the Lord wanted Calvary Chapel South Bay to reach out to the needs of more people in the community of South Bay, Los Angeles County: from Hermosa Beach to Torrance, from San Pedro to Wilmington; from Compton to Gardena. Steve recalls,

> One night after returning from a retreat, I went to bed. There was something different about this night. My heart was stirred, and I felt God wouldn't let me fall asleep. It was apparent God had something to say to my heart. Lying in my bed restless for hours, I finally reached over, grabbed my Bible, and started to read. God's Word just exploded in my heart, and every question and doubt about moving the ministry were now gone. I knew what God wanted, and it became crystal-clear what I had to do.

That night God ministered to Steve from Isaiah 54:2–4. Steve read it like this, with God speaking His words right into his heart.

> *"Enlarge the place of your tent"*: It's time to move to a bigger place so that I may do a bigger work.
> *"And let them stretch out the curtains"*: Steve, I will have other people come by your side to colabor.
> *"Do not spare; lengthen your cords"*: Strengthen your leadership!
> *"And strengthen your stakes"*: Steve, I am going to do a deeper work.

"For you shall expand to the right and to the left": The church shall reach out to the right and left of the Los Angeles 110 freeway.
"Do not fear, for you will not be ashamed!"

The property the church began looking at would fulfill all that God had promised to Steve. So the project began. The church placed an offer on a large building located on Vermont Blvd. in Gardena. It was a "backup offer" as the property was already in escrow with another company. Almost immediately it fell out of escrow. Now the questions began to arise. Would there be enough money? Would the zoning allow a church? One by one God began to move the mountains that were in the church's path.

The asking price for the building was several million dollars. Calvary Chapel South Bay was able to get a loan without any cosignatory and for the full amount needed. Furthermore, the building happened to be in an M2 zone, the only zone that allows churches to build without a use permit change. Another big miracle came as people from the church went to the planning department to look for help with the building plans. While two of the pastors were in line talking about the property, the architect who drew the original plans was standing behind them in the line. The chances of this happening are a million to one! After overhearing the pastors' conversation, the architect offered to help with the layout and answer any questions that they had.

The story continues to get better. As the pastors stepped up to the counter, the director of the planning department came out of his office to help them. He told them that all they would need was a plot plan instead of the more intricate plans, which they thought would be needed. This saved about a year in planning time and thousands upon thousands of dollars. The project was under way, and it was evident that God was in every step taken.

Then came the obstacles.

Then came the obstacles. Were there enough parking stalls? Was the ground being built on contaminated? When church representatives took their plot plan to the county offices for parking verification, they were told that they needed twice as many stalls than what they had. However, when they went for a second opinion with another company, they found that it was not that way. The parking stalls were submitted, and no further examination was required.

Then came the issue with the ground. It was thought that the ground was contaminated, so test samples were ordered. The results came back indicating that the ground was contaminated with solvent! Normally at this point, most people would walk away from the deal. But Steve and the board knew God wanted them there, so they called the previous owners to determine what they would do with this problem. Their answer of "nothing" was not what they wanted to hear. Again the church went to prayer.

The very next day, the previous owners called Steve back. They informed him that they had changed their position and would not only help with the cleanup costs but also pay for further testing and cleanup of any toxic spills. In addition, they also agreed to extend escrow for two more weeks (which saved the church $1,200 in interest fees). Even in the things that Steve and the church thought were obstacles, God was with them.

> *Each person is a beautiful demonstration of the work that the Master Builder does in each one of our lives.*

God also provided through the workers, vendors, and suppliers. He brought two men who were trained to run the phone lines to volunteer their services for free. The church received discounts on rental equipment; scissor lifts for half price; panels at no charge; and concrete, steel structuring, and plumbing at cost. God also provided carpenters, block layers, masons, painters, and journeymen to do the electrical at prices the church could afford, saving hundreds of thousands of dollars!

On Saturdays for almost nine months, 100 to 200 people from the church body gathered together and formed a work crew. God provided above and beyond what anyone could have ever asked for or imagined from Him. Steve recalls God using this project in his life:

The building project was just another breaking of my life. It was a massive project. It was so much more than just a building. What we built was a home and a place that we could dedicate and use for the glory of God. Furthermore, it was important to realize that the church of Jesus Christ is made up of people, not material things. It's the people, by the grace of God, who make our church what it is today. Each person is a beautiful demonstration of the work that the Master Builder does in each one of our lives.

In addition to building the new Calvary Chapel South Bay facility, the Lord also allowed Steve and the congregation to build relationships. The congregation in South Bay became a closer-knit family.

The searching for, finding, and building of a new church became a story of faith, vision, obstacles, provisions, building relationships, and, above all, God's faithfulness. Steve learned during this time that a church is never about a building or a piece of land, but rather about how God, the Master Builder, works and builds within His people. And that is what God did. He worked in the congregation, leaders, and staff of Calvary Chapel South Bay.

In the third chapter of Nehemiah, the families in Israel worked next to one another in order to rebuild the city walls of Jerusalem. Steve and his congregation saw a living picture of this as their work days brought out both families and individuals, at times up to 200 people who worked side by side in order to build this church. They all came—the young and old, single and married. Everyone came out and each did their part, having one common goal—to love and serve God.

It really was a bittersweet experience when the work was done. We really did become a closer family . . . a family that came together during hard times and tired moments to work together to build a home.

What we thought would be a simple building project with concrete work and framing turned out to be a building project of flesh and spirit. God, the Master Builder, decided to do a greater work, building in the hearts of individuals, families, and ministries. The Lord used this building project as a time to build faith, vision, and relationships and to teach us how to sacrifice. He wanted us to realize that He is always faithful and that where He guides, He provides. Looking back, we now see the real work of His Spirit. It was not in the way He provided for the buildings but rather what He did deep inside of each of our own personal lives. What He really wanted to build was in the people. The Bible says in the first verse of Psalm 127, "Unless the LORD builds the house, they labor in vain who build it." It was God who built the house, and we can declare, "Great is *His* faithfulness!"

Chapter 9

COMPLETING THE WORK

How can God use a man like Steve Mays? He was once a heartbeat from hell and is now being used for the kingdom of heaven. What happened in his life? The answer is divine intervention. The apostle Paul said, "And you He made alive, who were dead in trespasses and sins, in which you once walked according to the course of this world . . . among whom also we all once conducted ourselves in the lusts of our flesh, fulfilling the desires of the flesh and of the mind, and were by nature children of wrath, just as the others. But God, who is rich in mercy, because of His great love with which He loved us, even when we were dead in trespasses, made us alive together with Christ (by grace you have been saved)" (Ephesians 2:1–5).

After more than 30 years in the ministry, Steve has realized the work is really never done. He continues to battle with severe sleep apnea and other physical ailments. In fact, at the writing of this booklet, he fractured a disk in his back, which demanded immediate surgery. This removed him from the church for 90 days, to recover on his back at home.

Steve is also in the midst of yet another building project as God has given more property to the ministry of Calvary Chapel South Bay. He knows for a fact it is the grace of God that has seen him through, and it will be the grace of God that will continue to see him through.

Today Steve realizes that when God ministered to his heart from Isaiah 54 about the new church building, it was far beyond the building project. It was more than the material building God wanted to establish. God wanted to build up the people of Calvary Chapel South Bay, its staff and leadership, the community, and the world.

According to Isaiah 54, anytime a tent is stretched, the center poles must be strengthened, the ropes lengthened, and the stakes driven deeper into the ground. God wants His people to *expect* great things from Him and to *attempt* great things for Him. God uses ordinary people to do extraordinary things. God also wants His people to be willing: willing to get involved, willing to recognize a need, and willing to finish. God will do the rest.

The passage in Isaiah 54 is not a thing of the past but the vision for the future. Perhaps you feel, like Steve did, that there is no fruit in your life or that the trials are to no avail. Take heart! God has not forgotten you. His message is still the same. It is a message of love and forgiveness. Like God has done and will continue to do for Steve, God wants to bring down the mountains in your life and rise up the valleys. He wants to make the crooked paths in your life straight and longs for you to let go of the past. You can't change it or redeem it, but you can move on. It's time to let go of the baggage and fulfill the purpose for which God has called you.

Steve has learned God's command to sing and rejoice, even in the midst of trials. For you, that means singing even if you did not bear good fruit and rejoicing even if you feel like you have not succeeded.

In Isaiah 54:6, God says that He has called you! Regardless of your state—feeling barren, desolate, or simply that God is being silent—you must recognize He wants to do a new work. God wants you to forget the past and to no longer be afraid. He will do a new work, and you will not be ashamed! This is a lesson Steve has learned and will continue to learn.

It's time to let go of the baggage and fulfill the purpose for which God has called you.

Enlarge your tent. Make room for Him. He is the Lord of the harvest and is ready to work. He is also asking for you to lengthen your cords and make more time for Him. He is calling you and each of His children to have a self-sacrificing love, a greater love, and a love that reaches out and embraces a dying world. This also means having more faith. He's calling you to go deeper in your faith, a faith that is able to strengthen the faith of others.

God is also asking each of His children to strengthen the stakes in their personal lives. God longs for a deeper commitment. Drive your stakes deeper into the foundation of His Word. In the busy-ness of daily life, it is easy to get encumbered about many things and forget the one thing that is most needful—to sit still before the Lord and listen to what He would say to you.

Over the years, Steve has realized that listening to God isn't an easy thing to do. Three characters of the Bible—David, Moses, and Ruth—had to learn this difficult lesson in their lives. God said to Moses, "Stand still my servant, and you will see the salvation of God." To David, God spoke, "Be still my son, and know that I am God." To Ruth, God said, through Naomi, "Sit still my daughter until He has accomplished the work." God will help you apply these three simple yet difficult tasks to your day: Stand still, be still, and sit still, for He will complete the good work!

Steve Mays has made a choice for life in Christ Jesus. The Lord, according to His promise, will likewise complete the work that He has begun in Steve.

Looking back over his life, Steve understands better what the author of the book of Hebrews and the great apostle Paul said: "Jesus [is] the author and finisher of our faith" and "Being confident of this very thing, that He who has begun a good work in you will complete it until the day of Jesus Christ" (Hebrews 12:2; Philippians 1:6).

These promises of God are certainly evident in Steve Mays' life.

Conclusion

A NOTE FROM STEVE MAYS

In the book of Isaiah, God promises He will give beauty for ashes (Isaiah 61:3). This is my life in a nutshell. All the junk and hard times I went through as a child and young adult have been exchanged for a beautiful life of God's peace and happiness. I cannot say that I fully understand why God allowed all of those things to happen, but I can say that each time, through each circumstance and each trial, He was faithful to bring me through. God has been so good to me for the more than 30 years that I have been walking with Him, and I know He will continue to be faithful. It hasn't always been easy, but with Him as my strength, I have made it through each trial.

This story of mine is just an example of how God works in lives so that He might be glorified. If you don't have a personal relationship with Jesus Christ, then that's where you need to start. Accept Him as Lord and Savior of your life. Then you can experience and enjoy a Spirit-filled life full of the love of God.

My life testifies that God can take someone with nothing—someone sleeping in the gutter—and make something beautiful out of his or her life. Thirty years ago I would never have dreamed that my life could be used like this. To think that at one time I had nothing, not even a warm meal. And now I am rich, not in material things, but in God's peace, joy, and service. I have a wife whom I cherish and who loves me dearly, two wonderful children, and two grandchildren who are all the joy of my heart. Furthermore, God has given me a staff and congregation who are the best people a pastor could ever ask for.

My prayer for you after reading this booklet is that you would allow God to touch your life in any way He wishes. He wants to do a work in your life. Will you allow Him to?

If you are a believer and are facing difficult times, be encouraged that God will always be faithful to bring you through your times of trial, just as He has done for me. If you are a pastor or church leader, don't despise the days of small things. Each season in your life is a stepping-stone for God to build on. It might not happen overnight. I think I am the last of the 12 guys whom Pastor Chuck Smith wrote about in his book titled *Harvest* to get a church building of my own. Yet at the same time, you need to know it is not about church buildings. It's for God to get ahold of each one of us so that He might take His rightful place in our lives as Lord. Don't quit and don't give up. God has a plan much bigger than you can ever imagine. He will do exceedingly, abundantly above all you can ask or imagine (Ephesians 3:20). Be faithful to do your part, and God will do His.

If you do not know Jesus Christ or are not certain that you have a personal relationship with Him, I would be amiss if I didn't give you the opportunity to ask Him to come into your life. Yes, right now you can pray a simple prayer and ask Him to be the Lord of your life. It doesn't matter what you have done in the past; if God can love Steve Mays and make something out of my life, then He can and will do the same for you.

Two thousand years ago, God sent His Son in the form of a man to come to earth and to die on the cross for my sins and your sins. God knew then the life that you would lead and the things that you would do. Yet He still gave up His only Son to die so that you might live. I am not talking about religion or rules but simply an intimate relationship with Him. It is time for you to surrender your heart and give God an opportunity to transform your life from ashes into something beautiful.

If you would like to ask Jesus Christ into your heart, then simply pray this prayer right where you are:

Dear Jesus, I admit that I am a sinner, and I ask you to forgive me of my sins. I ask you to come into my heart and fill me with the power of your Holy Spirit. Write my name in the Book of Life. Help me right now to surrender *all* to your authority. Fill me with your joy, and open my eyes to see your love. In Jesus name, Amen.

If you prayed this prayer, I would like to be the first to welcome you to the family! Angels are rejoicing in heaven over you! I am also rejoicing with you, because I know what it feels like to be set free from the power of shame and guilt.

Finally, I would like to send you a Bible and help you get plugged in to a good Bible-teaching church in your area. Please call the Calvary Chapel South Bay church office or visit our website at www.ccsouthbay.org. God bless you!

Epilogue

CALVARY CHAPEL
SOUTH BAY INFORMATION

Steve Mays is an international speaker and the senior pastor of Calvary Chapel South Bay in Los Angeles, California. Steve first came to the Lord in 1970 when he attended Calvary Chapel Costa Mesa and became part of the revival that swept through Southern California during that period. Taken quite literally from the gutter by the miraculous workings of the Lord, he was brought up in the faith under the instruction of Pastor Chuck Smith, senior pastor of Calvary Chapel Costa Mesa and the founder of the Calvary Chapel movement.

Within a few years after his conversion, Steve planted and started several house ministries, which helped individuals get off the streets, out of drugs, and into God's Word. In 1978, Steve started and became the senior pastor of a new Calvary Chapel in the city of Cypress. By January of 1980, the Lord had led him to Calvary Chapel South Bay, where he has been the senior pastor ever since.

Calvary Chapel South Bay had approximately 50 members when Pastor Steve first arrived. The original church started with a 6,000-square-foot building and grew to a facility with 26,000 square feet. The church remained there until June of 1998 when it outgrew the facility and moved to its current location only a mile away.

Today, Calvary Chapel South Bay is home to more than 6,000 adults and over 1,700 children who attend Sunday services. The campus has four buildings compiling close to 200,000 square feet of building space on 10½ acres of property. There are more than 100 ministries operating within Calvary Chapel South Bay that reach throughout the Los Angeles area and the world.

Steve Mays has become a well-known conference speaker and has a national radio broadcast called "Light of the Word." Steve assists Pastor Chuck Smith with the Calvary Chapel Outreach Fellowship (CCOF) organization, which oversees and affiliates all Calvary Chapel churches worldwide. He is also a chaplain with the Los Angeles County Sheriff's Department; a chaplain for the Community Crisis Hotline; and the director of Calvary Chapel Bible College extension campus located in South Bay. Steve is a graduate of Azusa Pacific University and holds two master's degrees in ministry and divinity.

In addition to his responsibilities as senior pastor of South Bay, Steve has been blessed with a wonderful family. Steve has been married to his wife Gail for more than 30 years. Steve and Gail have two children, a son Nathan and a daughter Heather, and two grandchildren.

For more information, contact:
Calvary Chapel South Bay
19300 S. Vermont Avenue
Gardena, California 90248
(310) 352-3333
Websites:
www.ccsouthbay.org
www.lightoftheword.org

MATERIALS AVAILABLE BY STEVE MAYS

CHOICES
Who Will You Serve?

We all make CHOICES . . .

In fact, life is full of choices. Have you ever made a bad choice? Was the outcome filled with pain, despondency, or a feeling of failure? Choices are your responsibility, but the choices made today will determine the outcome of your future.

Using the Old Testament book of Joshua as his text, Pastor Steve Mays takes an in-depth look at the choices that knock at the door of your life daily and the impact those choices have in life. Furthermore, Steve will give practical counsel to challenge and encourage you to make good and effective decisions. Immediately you will discover how good decisions will bring deeper dedication to the Lord, which will result in greater joy and peace.

We encourage you to visit Calvary Chapel South Bay's website at www.ccsouthbay.org if you want to order additional copies of *Heartbeat from Hell* or Steve Mays' book, *Choices*. If you wish to receive additional information and audio messages by Steve Mays (video/audiotape, CD packages, and Bible studies), these are also available online or you may contact us by calling 310-352-3333 or by writing to:

Calvary Chapel South Bay
19300 S. Vermont Avenue
Gardena, CA 90248